deer camp dictionary

Hunting Terms Of EnDEERment

greg nachazel

RHODES & EASTON

Traverse City, Michigan

This book is meant to be humorous. The publisher will not be held responsible for any misuse or misinterpretation of its contents. In other words, laugh and have fun, but don't hold Rhodes & Easton responsible for your lives and the choices you make.

Publisher's Cataloging-in-Publication Data
Nachazel, Greg
     Deer Camp Dictionary / by Greg Nachazel
  Traverse City, MI : Rhodes & Easton, c. 1997.
        p.   ill.   cm.
     ISBN: 0-9649401-4-0
     1. Deer hunting – Humor. 2. Hunting – Humor.
     3. American wit and humor. I. Title
SK301.N33   1997
639.11'7357

Printed in the United States of America

99 98 97 ☺ 5 4 3 2 1

Joan Marie:

I turned the illustrations into a publisher, now marry me or I'm joining the Benedictine Monks in Saint Cloud.

Love, Greg

Contents

Acknowledgements

Without the vision, patience and perseverance of Mark Dressler, these concepts would still be in an old brown sketch book collecting dust.

bait pile
\bāt pī(ə)l\ *n.*

Discipline, stealth, fierce determination, and about $1,800 worth of buck vegetables come together to create that magic moment of shooting a deer while it's innocently eating breakfast.

[1]**browse line (natural)**
\braůz līn*n.*

A naturally occurring sign in the forest, the browse line can show you how tough the winter was by examining the height and intensity of winter nibbling on edible tree parts.

[2]**browse line (unnatural)**
braủz līn*n.*

As that great florescent orange wave (not a red tide) sweeps up into the game areas for hunting season once a year and fresh air and exercise bring on huge appetites, restaurants are quick to offer smorgasborgs or, as we note here, unnatural browse lines.

buck fever
\bək fē-vər\ *n.*

A hunter's illness which takes many forms, buck fever can cause even a seasoned, well-prepared hunter to forget even the simplest of things... like shooting a trophy buck right in front of him.

buck lure

\bək lü(ə)r\n.

Hunters relish the night before opening day for many reasons, but the ceremonial blowing up of the camp's inflatable doe is a special spiritual moment. (They make great lures, too.)

buck pole
\bək pōl\ *n.*

An ageless camp tradition, the buck pole is where successful hunters gather their kills for all to admire. By season's end the poles of serious camps are crowded with trophy bucks. Hunters are quick to point out the entry wounds behind the front shoulders. Some years at season's end the camp's sharpshooters gather to remember better years.

buckasaurus rex

\bək-ə-sȯr-əs rəks_n._

Unarmed, hope that you never meet one in rutt. These bucks carry the most primitive whitetail genes: They are fearless, oversexed monarchs of the forest with bad attitudes who show no mercy and never forget a hunter with bad breath.

camouflage

ka-mə-fläzh,-fläj\\ *n.*

Seasoned, expert hunters (and you know who you are) know how to apply the native craft of camouflage and disguise themselves as sleeping tree stumps in order to get close to those elusive trophy bucks.

deer blind
\di(ə)r blīnd\ *n.*

An expression which refers to warning signs about a dangerous whitetail deer condition. Thousands of deer are afflicted with this blindness each year and become oblivious to their surroundings, just like people.

deer camp
\di(ə)r kamp_n._

That ageless expression which calls to mind those earliest of memories of fun with your uncles and cousins in the fall forests of the north.

deer crossing

di(ə)r krȯ-sing\\ *n.*

A natural location to take up a shooting position, marked deer crossings are favorite places for many hunters at dusk and dawn when whitetails are very active.

drive hunt
\drīv hənt\ *v.*

A great deer hunting tradition. The drive hunt stirs the souls of most hunters, especially those inspiring words, "Gentlemen, start your engines." And off you go – happy hunting!

first light
\fərst līt*v.*

A pre-dawn technique of alerting other hunters to the location of your morning hunting spot. This can prevent other early morning hunters from ground checking (see pg. 39) you using their sound shooting skills (see pg. 73). This is a case where smoking could save your life.

fresh droppings
fresh dräp-ings*n.*

Occasionally while roaming your favorite hunting grounds you will come across fresh droppings. Their size, texture, and moisture content can tell you a lot about your prey.

fresh sign
\fresh sīn*n.*

When your hunting party returns to your preferred spot in the forest to find little signs that read "Posted" all over the place, rest assured. Off-season research has proved that this area is teeming with wildlife. Happy hunting, and make sure you show your kill to the landowner.

ground check
\graŭnd chek_n._

The age old woodland craft of getting a close-up look at a deer's head by blasting it. Usually it was just too far away. Sometimes it was near shrubbery that seemed to hide the antlers that kinda looked like they were there. Take this deer in for a successful hunter patch anyway! (see pg. 77)

gut pile
\gət pī(ə)l\ *n.*

Few things are more impressive than finding a nice, neat, orderly pile of guts on the ground on opening day. It is proof positive that the hunter did not gut shoot the deer or cause it unneeded suffering, other than not being able to finish his breakfast.

hunker down

hən-kər **daủn***v*.

Nature provides great natural conceal-ment in its old burned out pine tree stumps left over from the old logging days. All that is required is for the hunter to hunker down into one and wait for The Big One to walk by.

hunter's ball
hənt-ərs **bȯl***n.*

During the hunting season, and typically on Saturday nights, you will find hunters dancing together to the Blaze Orange Hunters Waltz at the unlikeliest of places, as well as local dance halls.

hunter's orange
hənt-ərz **är**-inj*n.*

Don't even think of going off into the forest on opening day without an orange in your possession. It is in violation of the law during hunting season. You could be searched, arrested, fined, and imprisoned. Tangerines will not keep you out of trouble.

jam

\jam\ *n.*

Few moments during your deer hunt are more worthy of a photograph. A jammed rifle typically occurs while that twelve point is in your sights. Careful selection of your ammo can prevent some jams.

mounting

maunt-ing*v.*

Taxidermists will tell you there are plenty of impressive options to mounting your buck; however, this is not one of them. Before tagging your kill, make sure he is really down for good.

mullein

məl-lən\\ *n.*

The true hunter's friend, mulleins are nature's own pre-moistened towelette. Many a hunter, being overcome with the majesty of the forest and the internal combustion of a hearty camp meal, has found himself seeking relief without the benefit of his favorite bathroom tissue. The leaves are fuzzy and conveniently shaped to fit even the hairiest ass in the woods.

opening day

\ōp-(ə-)ning **dā***n.*

Most hunters like to fortify themselves
the day before the season opens by
loading up before the big event –
just like marathon runners do.
Bottoms up and happy hunting early
in the morning!

pit blind

\pit blīnd\ *n.*

Whitetail deer rarely take notice of a hunter in a well thought out, concealed position. The pit blind can be assembled virtually anywhere and is very effective.

poaching

pōch-ing*v.*

All too often the big business of poaching goes on unimpeded while elaborate schemes and stake-outs are orchestrated to catch harmless hunters without an orange.

road hunting
\rōd hənt-ing\v.

Cram as many hunters, rifles, beverages, and ammo as you can into an old pickup and drive the back roads while you all discuss where to stop and hunt – till most of the daylight is gone. Occasionally deer tracks crossing the road are examined for their freshness. Expect to do a lot of this at camp.

rub (not a scrape)
rəb*v.*

A wise hunter takes note of these signs: a small sapling rubbed and broken says, "Little buck in the meadow"; a large, mature tree that is mutilated and savagely torn up says, "Get the hell out of the woods... fast!"

runway

rən-wā*n.*

Odd as it may sound, hunters often take up shooting positions near runways, sometimes even right on them. However, be careful – the deer are frequently travelling real fast. And don't tamper with the landing lights.

scope eye
skōp ī*n.*

How do you prove to your wife you
actually took your rifle out of its case?
Simply hold your rifle loosely against
your shoulder and rest the eyepiece on
your eyebrow, and then fire! **Bang!!**
There you have it – a nice circular gash
around your eye. Go ahead – make up
a hunting story. Think of the sympathy.

scrape (not a rub)
skrāp*v.*

Not to be confused with a similar buck-in-rutt activity designed to mesmerize the does in the neighborhood, the small scrape on the ground may only attract oversexed wood ticks, while a large, impressive scrape can accumulate herds of does anxious to make friends with the big buck.

shining
shī-ning*v*.

A popular felonious hunting method used very late at night. "Hunters" use million candle power spotlights to blind trophy bucks out eating in the starlight. They then blast them and enter them in buck pole contests. Hmmm...

sound shooting
saund shüt-ing*v*.

The woodland art form of shooting deer in near or total darkness. This skill will take you years – as well as cases of ammo – to perfect. Beginners should be very sure everyone at camp is inside playing poker and that no one is outside processing a mullein (see pg. 51.) (Remember to close your eyes when shooting or the muzzle flash will spoil your night vision.)

still hunting
\stil hənt-ing\ *n.*

This is a special hunter's greeting used between hunters in the woods many weeks after the season has ended. When you meet another hunter, just shout out, "Hey, still hunting?"

successful hunter patch

\sək-**ses**-fəl **hənt**-ər **pach***n*.

In the final analysis, after all the handed down knowledge, learned and honed skills, and noble ideals, the hunter needs great luck, fortunate timing, and something to shoot at. Of all the rewards for a great hunt, the one that lasts year after year is the successful hunter patch awarded to any hunter willing to bring his or her kill in for an inspection.

swamp buck
\swämp bək\ *n.*

Craftiest of all whitetails, the swamp buck has learned how to adapt to loss of habitat, to include natural wetlands, and still remain the most elusive trophy in the forest.

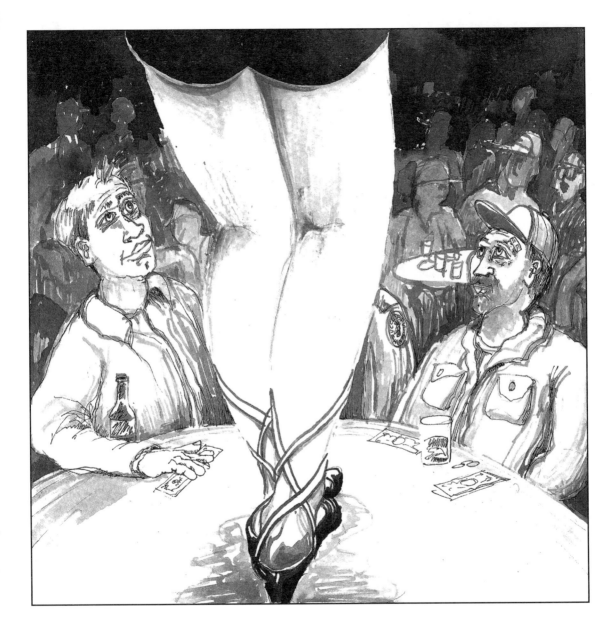

tenderloins

ten-dər-lȯinz*n.*

Hunters as a whole look forward to that special time together feasting on tenderloins. In a recent national survey of deer camps, 9 out of 10 whitetail hunters agreed that tenderloins were their favorite choice of meat.

tight shot group
\tīt shät grüp*n.*

At deer camp and in hunter's parlance, a tight shot group usually refers to the first set of shots poured that particular day. A calm head and pouring in between breaths can guarantee a tight group.

track soup
\trak süp*n*.

At the end of a long day of hunting, without anyone dragging in a deer, hunters gather at the pot; no matter what's cooking, it's just track soup tonight.

tree blind

\trē blīnd\ *n.*

A tree blind can offer the hunter a distinct sight advantage. Whitetail deer just don't pay close attention to who or what is in the trees. They only notice you after you have fallen down.

trespassing

tres-pəs-ing*v*.

These signs alert hunters to the presence of deciduous trees called Tres, which can emit foul, poisonous odors. The No Trespassing signs simply mean hunting in this area is safe at this time.

true north

\trü nȯ(ə)rth *n.*

An expression used by hunters familiar with land navigation. True north is a direction on a map, while magnetic north is altogether quite different, depending on just how lost you are.

two tracks
\tü traks*n.*

Otherwise known as 'seasonal roads,' two tracks allow hunters access into remote wildlife areas where hunting the secret places in the forest can be enjoyed, and mud pits, where trying to get the vehicle unstuck can be experienced.

zeroing in

\zē-rō-ing **in**\v.

Don't wait till there is a buckasaurus rex (see pg. 21) in your sights to zero in your rifle. Finding out you can't hit anything in front of you can be disappointing. Besides, zeroing in may be all the shooting you get.

Ordering Page

You will need more Deer Camp Dictionaries if:

- Your camp has more than one outhouse.
- You were unable to readily find mulleins at camp.
- You want a sincere "gee, thanks" at Christmas.
- You used all of your newspapers to start a camp fire.

To order, call 800-706-4636 and we will send you as many copies as you would like for $8.95 each. Order two or more books, and we will pay the shipping charges (otherwise add $2 for shipping). Visa or MasterCard accepted, or send a check for $10.95 to:

Rhodes & Easton
P.O. Box 192
Traverse City, MI 49685-0192
Volume discounts available for multiple quantities
☺